Emily
Lovely,

Keep travelling

Below Flodden

Noel Hodgson

Noel Hodgson

The Reiver Press

The Reiver Press
2 Woodhouse, Shilbottle, Alnwick,
Northumberland NE66 2HR

First published in Great Britain by The Reiver Press, 2003

A CIP catalogue record for this book is available from the British Library

ISBN 0-9545181-0-1

Printed in Great Britain by Antony Rowe Ltd,
Chippenham, Wiltshire

This collection is dedicated to
Judith and our children, Robynne and Guy,
and to my mother,
indomitable spirit that she is.

Also,
to the memory of George Neighbour, friend,
who believed in it from the beginning.

I wish to acknowledge the following people
for their valuable contributions:

Ken Smith, Bob Smith, Jimmy Keen and Mike Hope
for their photographs.

Colleagues and friends for their encouragement.

Judith, Mother and Uncle Tommy
for their approval and support.

Fred Dyson, for his guidance and inspiration.

Bill Grisdale, for his creative and technical skills.

Dave White, editor, who has nurtured this project
with skill and care from start to finish.

And all the characters and personalities
whom I endeavoured to portray,
especially those no longer around
to learn from these pages
just how highly I thought of them.

Like a lone hunter following the scent of wonder,
I've trekked across the face of north Northumberland
many times to leave this trail of poems.
I hope their impressions are marked and clear enough
for readers to follow without too much effort.

Rain, water pouring down the walls;
A century of harsh winters has disfigured them.
Now the stone is scarred a little more.

Replacing a broken pane, a sheet of polythene
Is flapping in the wind. At a doorstep,
A broom's handle lying in a pool.
Beyond a gate, a rubbish heap still smouldering,
Gusts throwing out smoke, angrily whisking
It away. On dull, wet roofs cling small islands
Of lichen; dry, they turn a bright yellow-orange.

After rain, the sun suddenly breaking through,
Brightly varnishing every surface.
Reappearing, birds splashing and flustering
Around dripping spouts. From an umbrella
Of trees, sheep treading out in line
Over glistening grass.

Across a glossy, soaked yard, the tramp
Of boots entering a dusty, dingy hemmel.
Soon, the rumble of the turnip cutter,
Like a drum, bidding beasts on straw to rise
And shuffle towards worn wooden troughs.

Wind tugging, the fire swiftly stirs,
Flame spreading, igniting flame, wringing out
Thick trails of grey-black smoke.

After rain, beneath the sun's spreading arms,
Another scene unfolds again upon the solid stance
Of this coarse-faced, willing old farmstead.

For many years this farmstead was home and central to my growing.
The warm sandstone buildings were a playground of countless hideouts, full of
contraptions and smells, and with a powerful atmosphere of past and present use.
Their structure remains solid, tenacious and alive.

After breakfast
Colin rides out on horseback,
Taking the steep track
Onto the moor.
Concerned by clouds
He wears an unsure look.

Above a single oak tree
Rooks circle noiselessly.
In the cold morning air
The pony pants,
Its hot breath steaming
As it climbs the path
Between bracken and gorse.

On the hill top they pause;
Now Colin sees some of his flock
Beyond the pond.

Suddenly, a flash of sunlight
Sweeps across the water.
Upon the skyline
A transmitter mast glints;
A silver skeleton.

Moving on,
Colin rides past
A solitary stone
With ring marks scored towards
The moon.

Many a morning from the cottage window at West Weetwood, I watched Colin James, a young shepherd, riding up the hill to look the sheep. Thinking about his journey and what lay up there was a way of going too; of my being there.

From hillsides
Water tumbles
Into streams,
Pouring from valleys,
Growing,
In a river
Winding northwards
Towards the
Sea.

Ancient river,
Between its banks
The blood of fighting generations
Drained from the land.
The water moves,
Reflects the sky
And the ghosts
Of many faces.

All flow to the river:

The young on branches
Above the current
With dreams of walking
On the water;
Lovers, hand in hand,
Silent, thoughtful,
Gazing at the motion,
Sensing in themselves
The pull of destiny;
Old ones with sticks,
Aware of death
And their drowning days,
Glancing at themselves
In the river
With arms outstretched
For something more
Than life.

*Inspired by Andrew Patton, an old farmer and war veteran, walking with two sticks
at the Linthaugh near Ford, by the river Till, taking his place in the continuing cycle
of this time-drawn scene.*

Beside the road,
A walled enclosure
Arched with trees
Marks Percy's mortal leap
At the battle of Hedgeley.

Across the highway,
Numbered like corpses,
Huge piles of timber lie
Stored in Scott's woodyard;
A thriving business built
By the stride of a bold,
Hard-working man.

Despite their divide,
Mounted, side by side
That fatal Spring day,
This redoubtable pair
Would have surely made
Far sterner allies than
The weak-chested lords,
Hungerford and Ros, whose
Flight from the field
Left proud Percy to suffer
His brave, exalted fall.

St Mark's Day, April 25th, 1464: Yorkist troops under Montague were intercepted by a Lancastrian force headed by Sir Ralph Percy. Deserted by his lords, Percy's death on horseback and his final words, that he had, at least, 'saved the bird in his bosom', have since become legend. No one now knows exactly what he meant by that and it remains something of a riddle. Perhaps he was referring to the fact that he remained honourable to the last. I like to think so anyway.

Andy Scott, a local woodman, saw his business prosper after moving to Wooperton, in 1959. His renowned strength of character and determination were key factors in his success.

The adjacency of the sites – Wooperton sawmill and Percy's Leap – and the tenacity of both individuals led to the poem's conjecture. Percy's Cross stands south of the mill, a lasting memorial to the doomed knight.

Thomas rolls over,
Leaves his bed.
Later, alone,
In a cold, grey dawn
He steers his boat
Across the cove.

One by one
He hauls up his creaves.
On the sea's horizon
The sun bulges
Large and red,
Like Thomas's hands,
Tossing small lobsters
Back into the water.

With wind, waves grow;

Standing tall,
Thomas feels the blow
Against his cheek.
Leaning towards land
He sees his father
Above the Heugh,
Angled towards his sheep.

Locally, bad weather from a south-easterly direction is said to be coming straight out of Howick Hole! I can't imagine the place without the Thompson family, who farm nearby and whose presence seems as natural as the cove itself.

She enters the arcade;
No one notices.
Solemn faces bound to
Adventures out in space,
On motorways,
In far off thrilling places.
Machines squawk, hiccup,
Whine and screech.
She takes out change
To feed a bandit;
Doesn't win.
No one speaks.
She strays outside,
Turning towards the harbour;
Moored boats rocking
In the wind and swell.
Cold, she slips into the
Olde Ship Hotel,
Buys a toasted sandwich,
A glass of cider,
Sits down at the window,
No one there beside her.
Across the room two men
Play darts;
Another with a paper
Selects his bets.
Forlorn, she stares out
Across a grey stark sea;
An empty page,
Where life's regrets are seen,
Invisibly, from a dark
And silent edge.

*No one in particular. Just an empty face or two on a bleak day, on a cold street,
looking for distraction and crumbs of comfort.*

Across the rise of moor
The old shepherd
Limps towards his sheep,
Fleeces sagging from
Morning rain.

On the roadside below,
Empty horse boxes
Parked in line.
Out of sight,
Riders and hounds
Chase their prey.

Upon the moor
Once warm with bracken,
The fresh ploughed earth
Lies black and bare.
Where rock and bush
Have been uprooted,
Both hunter and herdsmen
Shall soon pass without trace.
And the fox,
No longer running for life,
May simply vanish in the dust
Of change.

Modern farming continues to alter the landscape and the effects are also apparent in
empty farm cottages as well as missing wildlife. One man's vision is another's loss!
Ironically, without hunting I believe the fox would have become an endangered species.

The last time I saw Roger
He was flying a kite
With his children.

His death has cut the string;

Now he floats above me,
Not as a shadow
But a merry lively thing.

Walking along the beach one afternoon I watched someone flying a kite. Roger, a close friend since school days, had died some weeks earlier in an unfortunate accident, while still only in his thirties. When I saw the kite I was reminded of the very last time I saw Roger alive, and the poem came almost spontaneously.

A shrill bell!
Morning break has ended.
Teachers whistle children into lines.
Hands out of pockets, ties straightened,
They file back into classes.

Once the doors are shut
And the yard has fallen quiet,
Birds sail down onto the cement
Seeking spillage of crisps,
Biscuits, sweets.

Soon, a lone boy appears,
Carrying an empty litter bin;
His punishment for forgetting
His PE kit.

Back on roof and branches
Birds watch him and wait,
But the sullen boy is unhurried,
Shambling and stooping slowly,
Disinterested in his menial task,
Unaware of his audience,
And the vast stage he commands.

*I later told the boy about the birds, and of myself watching him from a window.
And how God would have seen him too! He said he didn't believe in God. I said that
wouldn't exclude him and that He, the birds and I weren't impressed with his
performance.*

First for seconds every time,
Little Alan with his plate piled high
Returns to the table with the shine of a grin,
While Fleming, caught running, sent back to his place
Sits opposite him with a frown on his face.

"There's none left now; take your tray and go!"
The voice of authority, heard to obey.

As Fleming, miserably, gets up from his chair,
His glass falls suddenly, smashing on the floor!

Heads turn; a round of laughter fills the hall.
Sir is annoyed, pointing to the door:
"After you've swept up, boy, stand in the foyer!"

Gladly, girls and boys go out to play;
Upstairs in the staff room, teachers pour tea.

Between them, alone, Fleming stands in his place,
Head bowed, unsmiling, unable to see,
The Queen looking down, a glow on her face.

Beneath her, alone, life has sadly bestowed,
That for poor, wretched Fleming, fortune's his foe.

Winners and losers have a look about them. Fleming seemed to possess
that appearance and manner which served him no advantage.
Whatever became of him?

The fire draws,
Heating water.
Pained with arthritis,
She sits in an armchair
Gazing at flames.

Outside, in a March sun,
With a cold, ragged breeze,
He builds paddocks
For his lambing ewes.

Turning to the window
She sees hilltops, still white;
A robin, with finches, feeding
Around the bird table.

Inside the room
There is only the ticking
Of a grandfather clock,
And the hiss of a burning log,
Until she hears, once more,
His hammering at a post;
The heavy mell ringing in
Another season,
Keeping their years
Burning, still.

Good old neighbours. A stack of money in a biscuit box under the bed; Bible by the pillow; a garden of plenty. Little spent, little squandered.

Familiar in dark waistcoat and
Navy overalls, he tossed the bales
Across the stack. Sleeves rolled up,
His lean arm muscles tensed, gripping
A hay fork, swinging it skilfully;
Often his aim was perfect. And as
A bale fell exactly into place,
His face would lift with glee.

Under a dust-stained cap, his small
Eyes glinted and a toothless grin
Half-circled his long nose.

Frequently, his wry words kept us
Amused, cheering our day's toil.
Humour lined his image; though no
One's fool. With a canny eye he
Perceived men's ways in the manner
Of creatures, revealing folly
With merry truth.

Hard-working, he'd spit on his palm,
Eager to take his turn; sensitive to
Simple fears, sometimes frustration
Or hurt would scorch him, but never
Marred his heart's main strength:

Who would think of him in love's
Royal line? Yet each and every day,
Sitting at the tractor wheel,
Leaving the farm yard, he'd wave back
To his wife, standing at their cottage
Door, as lovers tend, unabashed,
'Til out of sight.

*George Ogle was a traditional farm worker, amusing to work alongside. As coarse as
any other among men, he lived with respect and was fearlessly devoted to his wife. At
the sound of a tractor she would peer out to see if it was him at the wheel.*

The battle was won;
We were glad to be trooping home
With joyful, singing hearts.

By a stream we stopped to rest
And, pulling off our clothes, splashed
Loudly into the cold brown water,
While Seth of Elsdon brooded, alone,
Leaning in the shade of a green oak tree.

On Flodden field he'd sprung in rage
To slay a slight, boy-faced Scot,
Yet before he heaved the lethal blow,
Seth suddenly saw the terror of the lad
In himself, and turned to fight another man.

For two dismal days we dragged the dead,
Piling them into deep, mud-stinking pits
And, finding the youth he'd spared,
Seth carried him away to bury him, decently,
Like a brother.

So there we were, happy in the small,
Sun-filled valley, soaking our sores,
Bathing our grubby white bodies,
When a piper struck up a merry tune
And we, laughing, skipped out naked
To romp and stomp across the ground,
While Seth of Elsdon, frozen still
Between a mother and her son, stayed
Leaning in the shade of a green oak tree.

Just south of Wooler, entering Langleeford, is a place called Skirl Naked. The name has been connected, plausibly, to victorious English soldiers returning from battle at Flodden, in 1513. Yet the name is much older and relates more accurately to its stark, exposed position. Happy Valley lies immediately downstream.

Behind the church
A twin headstone;
'Nancy Brodie and Mary Hall,
Died by accident,
January 30th, 1965'.

Saturday night;
Girls out dancing,
Seeking fun and meeting,
Maybe romance.

We never met,
But at that time, too,
Twenty years old,
Out drinking,
Making friends,
Sometimes with feeling.

How the stars
Direct and divert us,
Leading us one way
Or another.

Even now, introduced,
In this lonely graveyard,
Enclosed by budding trees
And hillsides,
What curious trail
Entreats me to follow them,
Beyond this place?

Who they were, and what tragedy might have occurred, left me curious; especially as the girls had been local and of my own age. I carried them away in my mind. After writing this poem, I later discovered that what I'd imagined was true; together, killed in a car crash, returning from a Saturday night dance at Haggerston.

Perched on rock, the raven turns
Its ice-black stare towards the ruin;
Stones webbed by nettle and weed.

Mind and memory blazing in its eye.

In the swoop of the hillside,
The morning sun slips into the valley.
Near the well, goats, hens, children playing;
Smells of peat smoke, fleece and blossom;
A pony sledge hiding in tall, green bracken.

Mind and memory flashing in its eye.

Winter wind sweeping the moor,
Charging the shield of boulders and trees,
Surrounding, striking the roof and walls.
Sun setting over distant Cheviots;
White, upturned bellies, freezing blue.

Mind and memory gleaming in its eye.

Perched on rock the raven turns
Its ice-black head towards the sound,
Fading cries; a shepherd's loss.

Odin's two ravens were named Hugin and Munnin; Mind and Memory. Indeed, ravens
once nested up beside Blawearie. Two generations of the Rogerson family lived there,
from 1841 until approximately 1915. After them came Bob and Doll Rutherford.
From 1930 the Faills, followed by the Middlemasses and, briefly, the Blacks, inhabited
the place. Before eventually being abandoned in 1941, it became used as a shooting
lodge. Robert Rogerson and his family were largely responsible for cultivating the spot.
The well water still tastes lovely today.
Story has it that a shepherd and his wife, from Old Botany nearby, both perished on the
moor, lost in a blizzard while searching for a missing cow. The animal is said to have
returned the following day.
The Cheviot hills also give their name to a breed of sheep.

Beyond the bay, the island castle on
Its mount of rock stands supreme, but
Less in substance than the wind-carved,
Sun-wrought priory ruin; walls
And pillars of reddened stone
The castle builders left untouched.

Treeless isle, where vikings, saints,
Kings and heroes have framed a history
That time-tabled visitors can feel, simply
In the silence of their bones.

Tourists come and go. And some,
Seeking enchantment, buy a cottage
To go on living in the picture of their dreams;
While in 'reservation' row, locals know:
'No one can fly', and fear little else
Than an empty boat or the omen of a wind
That can snap through stone.

Surrounded by a shiftless rhythm of wave and tide,
Nature suspends the isle between land and sea;
An aged hoary hand with
A witch's knobbly finger, pointing towards
The past and future, mysteriously enduring,
Like a rainbow's arch, set against
A changing sky.

Within the priory's ruin there remains an arch, known as the 'Rainbow'.
Under threat today from tourism and holiday homes, the life of the island's community
and traditions is dwindling.
Surely the future of the island ought to be as valued as its past?

Seated in a garden
Beside a pond,
Afternoon sun shining warmly.
Sounds beyond the reeds:
Fish, ducks, birds;
Elsewhere, a tractor,
Sheep protesting,
A dog barking.

On nearby leaf,
Butterfly and bluebottle,
Pausing,
Catching the glow
Of mid-summer.

Today, July 20th, 1984,
Across the moor at Rothbury,
Young Robbie's funeral.

Elsewhere,
Throughout this countryside,
Children being born,
Couples marrying,
Sorrow and joy undenied,
Insisting upon tears and laughter.

Here and there
Across this land,
Clouds passing overhead,
Days and years falling away,
Gardens growing and dying.

Loved and grieved,
Life is somehow gratified
By an occasional glimpse
Of wings and water,
And a sky that seems to listen.

The sad death of Robbie Snaith and the tranquillity of the walled garden deepened awareness of mortality and the gift of life. At such a time, in so perfect a setting, contemplation soared towards a higher place.

Lumps of sheep,
Scouring
Snow-plastered heather.

Their horned heads,
Black splotching
The whitescape.

Straggled
Whin bushes,
Writhing at stabs
Of icy wind.

Blank, dying sun,
Hanging itself
Behind the moor's
Blanched shell.

Hard-frosted snow turning moorland into a wilderness. An end-of-the-world feeling in the depth of winter; daylight short, startling, fragile.

Remembering my son's cry
In the middle of the night;
Holding him beside the window,
Seeing a bright yellow moon
Floating above the dark wave of the hill;
The sudden feeling of a moment given,
A moment destined to be embraced
With another:

Of a child in a bath,
A yellow duck,
Bobbing,
Holding our attention,
Drawn in wonder
To the miracle of space.

The magnificence of a moon lifted my dulled senses of interrupted sleep.
This night, in the shadow of a valley, his cheek against mine,
it seemed to play with us as we watched.

Together,
My children and I
At the fence on the hillside,
Picking crab apples.

Backs to an autumn breeze,
We select the best
For our bag.

Today, it's my daughter
Robynne's seventh birthday.

As she grows older,
Leaving her childhood
Behind her,
May she recollect events
As simple as this,
In making choices
Of her own.

A father's hope, extending from a happy autumn morning in the valley.
These occasions cost nothing but invested time. There is no right way
to bring up children, only wrong ways.

Here he comes,
The village king,
Strolling from The Percy Arms.
His cap tilted,
Head held tall,
Shoulders back.
"Afternoon, Bob," a voice hails him.
He stops, eyes twinkling,
A hearty grin.
"An' the same t'you, sir!"
He cries, stick in the air,
Then wanders on home
To his seat in the garden,
A white painted chair.

Now smoking,
Cross-legged,
Content in the sun,
His memory drifting
Into the hills –
The lamb's gasp,
The shears' grind,
The bite of the snare;
Good friends,
Good whisky,
His summons each year.

With wit and an inkling
He believes still in the moon,
In the honour of hands;
Gives gladly,
Envies no man,
Happiness his rule.

Bob Fairbairn was an old shepherd and a village character.
Full of life, he enjoyed it heartily, his head brimming with memories.
He remained as tough as hawthorn, until the very end.

Putting in potatoes
Mother had forgotten
Under the bed.

Dug over before winter
The soil crumbles easily
With every turn of the spade.

Father, with his new teeth,
Tells, in a matter of fact way,
Of an old friend's funeral,
And another farmer's malady.
At an age when friendships
Are frequently disappearing,
He voices the inevitable,
Without emotion.

When this summer is ending
And these plants are lifted,
What else might have grown
From these thoughts,
Safely tucked away
Within my mind?

Father died the following April. Mother still loves her garden.

With rain splattered blood
Streaming down his cheek
He leaves behind his dying brother,
Arrowed in the dark marsh mud.
Wild-eyed, he lurches forward
Behind his heavy, simple shield,
To avenge the folly of stolen victory
And flee the terror of a murderous field.

Axe swinging in frenzied fury
He hacks through an English line,
Escaping from the hideous crime
Of careless, ruthless butchery.
Running madly towards the Tweed,
Desperately he gasps for breath,
Only glancing back fearful to heed
Any who might be in foul pursuit.

From the mist of cannon smoke
Hurl riders wearing Stanley's cloak,
Brandishing swords already blooded,
And faces masked by a brutal stare.
In the wet, darkening, evening light
They chase across the sodden ground,
Howling as they close in on him,
No less a man than his dead king.

The battle of Flodden, September 1513, was actually fought at Branxton after the Scottish army was forced to move position. The conflict was very significant in shaping our history. The poem attempts, in grand manner, to underline how dreadful it must have been for individual men, loosely trained, their loving hearts overwhelmed by fear and the cry of duty.

He shuffled outside to pee,
The night black and frozen,
A wisp of moon and dull stars
Seemed too far away.

With breath clouding the icy air
His urine steamed into the drain.
Returning, he glanced eastwards
Thinking of his mother's letter,
Words of comfort without complaint.

Inside the hut he shivered to bed,
Third on the right beyond the door.
Side-hunched below the blankets,
He covered his head and trembled,
Knowing next night he'd move
A place closer to the stove.

Out of the chilling darkness
He heard the youngest one awake,
Coughing in the bunk above.
Nineteen years old tomorrow;
He imagined the lad's surprise,
Receiving three slices of bread
With cheese and sausage.

Restlessly, over the muffled
Sounds of snoring, sighing men,
The gift, like a distant glow,
Dwindled in his mind, until again,
Sleep's numb drag removed him.

t the entrance gate to Glendale School sit two lions which were constructed by Italian
risoners. These are all that remain of the Camp. Fritz Berthele, a local man, was
riginally a German P.O.W. who arrived in March, 1946. I asked Fritz for information
oout life in the camp and – in his correspondence with a friend, Otto Knapp, a fellow
risoner – came details of their experience; none more fascinating than the bed
tation which ensured each man gained a share of warmth by the stove – and the extra
ortion of food in honour of Otto's birthday. Otto's letter to Fritz was later printed in
Vooler At War', published by Glendale Local History Society.

Football
On a sloping pitch,
Both teams struggling
To control the ball.
Their ardent shouts
Flung by a hectic wind
Out to sea, lost like
Gulls' startled cries
In a commotion of waves
Clapping loudly onto
Dark shore rocks.

Ahead,
Dunstanburgh castle's
Tombstone ruins propping
Up a cloud-canvassed sky.
On its bleak, basalt crag,
What ambitions lay within
Lancaster's churlish gaze?

Before
The ball is retrieved,
I liken all to a greater
Passing game, enjoyed at
Leisure by fit and fair,
Somewhere in the bay
Between mind and foot.

Dunstanburgh castle was built by Thomas, Earl of Lancaster, around 1313. He was nicknamed 'Churl' by Piers Gaveston, favourite of Edward II. The disloyal Thomas was executed in 1322.

The ball was often being sought, and my mind would wander from the pitch, delighting in the surrounding scenery. I only played for Craster for half a season before returning to rugby at Alnwick, but it left its mark. After folding, in the mid-1980s, the village team re-formed in 1991 and now play at Dunstan on a flatter pitch. Consequently, there'll be fewer opportunities for players to gaze.

Under a stark, afternoon sky
The helmet of the hill
Glows in low, raw sunlight.

Like a tribesman standing on its crest
I see the joining of valleys below;
The Bowmont running into the Glen,
Widening westwards towards the Till;
Rivers crowned in earlier times by acts
Of gathering and settlement.

Hunched hawklike in the chill breeze,
I hover towards the tumbled outer wall
Of the top's once ancient fort,
Spying the glint of a jet fighter
Rising from Milfield Plain.

As the roar passes I drop down,
Scampering like a wild goat
To the cover of oak trees which hair
The northern slope of the hill.
Here, warmer, out of sight,
Like a monk in the quiet hour
Before darkness falls,
I dwell, once more, upon Gefrin's ground,
Pondering with praise and awe,
The binding of this epic
Crossing place.

The prehistoric camp site on Yeavering Bell was the largest in the region. Gefrin is the
old name for this area, where King Edwin built his palace in the 7th century. It was here
that Paulinus converted and baptised, in the river Glen. The name Gefrin signifies a
place of goats. Today, wild goats still roam the hills around here.
This poem is for Fred, a friend, whom I once accompanied onto the hill. Although blind,
he will, with his extraordinary vision, perceive more than is said.

Heading into the hills
Beyond the linn,
Running like a fugitive,
Seeking not to hide
But idly roam, without having
To look over a shoulder
For the arrows and bullets
Of everyday demands,
Or the guilt of seeing them
Neglected.

Wandering into the Cheviots can be something of an escape from those routines and difficulties which burden us all from time to time. Entering the lonesome landscape of the border hills can clear the head and put into perspective the smallness of self.

A Suspension of Benifity
Hangs heavily upon
The stone-roofed building
And dismal, unkempt graveyard.
Yet, through the unlocked door,
The interior, vacant and sombre,
Remains dignified in repose.

Left lying on the prie-dieu,
Notes from the last service;
Blessings for a few,
Enfeebled and lost.

Apart from the thin wooden crucifix
Centred on the bare altar,
All other adornments are removed.

Above, overlooking the valley,
The solitary picture-window shows
The adoration of infant Jesus
In the stable of the inn;
Only now, the empty beer keg
For donations, standing beside
The visitors' book, seems less
Incongruous than at first.

Before leaving, as if a sign
Of unfaithfulness and undoing,
I wipe away the veil of cobweb
Finely traced between the head
And arms of the light, meagre cross.

Originating from the 13th century, this ancient church with dwindling use has survived centuries of threatened ruin and decay. Visiting here with my uncle, in April, 1999, we found within this solid edifice a breath of sanctity immovable and undeniable in the face of any demotion.

At the head of the valley, linked with an old trade route called Salter's Road, Alnham was once a significant and active spot. The tenuous connection between the keg and the inn is uncertain. Realistically, a keg is not as easy to break into or carry off as might be the more customary receptacle.

Snowflakes blowing;
Forwards, like giants,
Heave and strain
To win the ball,
While in the backs
We rub our hands
And shuffle our feet,
Braced to run.

From the touchline
A few home spectators,
Huddled in heavy coats,
Command our struggle.

All this a pantomime
Of muscle and grit
On a frozen Saturday
In December; players
As one, pitted against
A chilling, snarling
Monster.

Apparently, one Saturday, late morning, Dick Little from Mousen rang the club secretary to cry off from the Fourth Team's game that afternoon. When asked what was wrong, he replied that he'd been outside working that morning and it was too bloody cold! Such intrepid honesty struck me.

It was a fair tackle alright.
He must have twisted as he landed
For his right leg was bent below his left.

He lay on his back, gasping to hold
The pain, like a mother giving birth.
He got the usual cold-water sponge.

I reckoned it was cartilage.
His joint was so swollen it looked
Like it had been pumped up.

Bravely sitting, he grimaced as
Two big lads linked hands, making
Him a chair, and carried him gingerly
Off the pitch.

At the touchline a car drew up. Smartly,
Club officials slid him, like a corpse,
On to the back seat then drove away.

Our captain gathered us round,
Said it was bad luck on Derek, but now
With only fourteen men, we'd have to
Play even harder.

In the club house after the game,
We were together drinking pints,
When suddenly through the doorway
Derek hobbled in on crutches; an abject,
Desolate face, searching for consolement.

Instantly, someone hollered for him
To stop looking miserable; that
We'd won the match!

Even lamely, Derek had to grin.

In the club house, photos of players include my father, Duncan; uncle Tommy; brothers
Jim and Danny; nephews Andrew and Richard, and yours truly.

The boy waits,
Watching his sheep
Running towards him.
A Spring breeze curls his hair.
Calling his two collies
They drop immediately
To the ground,
Crouching; still.

The young man steps forward,
Raising his stick,
His face burnished by Summer sun.
Slowly, in an arc, he counts
The flock filing past.

The man lowers his stick,
Turning up his collar
Against an Autumn rain.
He checks his sheep,
Then turning away
Whistles his dogs.

The old shepherd
Leans upon the gate.
Dark against the snow
Both collies race to his side.
Gazing at a Winter sky
He squares his cap,
And circled in his eyes,
Years of caring reflect
An ageless light;
The glow of wisdom
At its gentlest.

Jack Douglas worked on the same farm for over fifty years, until he retired.
Throughout, with dignity and conscience, he sustained his interest and effort.
Only a great and humble man could have achieved such a feat.

Two trees crash down!
So now, scared from a wood,
Pheasants sail out
Above the heads of Gentlemen
With guns!

Shots ring out! Christmas here again!
And underfoot the creak of winter.
There the Shepherd,
Following his dog up the hill
Where cattle round a frozen trough
Wait for a hand to stone the ice.

In town the bustle and buying;
Shop windows glorious in day's dull light.
Parcels and people
Wrapped with good intentions,
Visions of a better world;
Safe for children among the leaves,
Victims for Great Herod's men.

Susan Maxwell was an eleven-year-old country girl who was abducted near Cornhill and later found murdered, in a wood, far from home, August, 1982.

Where is safe?

Not here,
Among the rocks,
Within the hollows and holes
Of these large outcrop boulders,
Where women and children
Scurried to hide while their menfolk below
Defended their homes from the invaders' torch and sword.

Nowhere is truly safe
From a ceaseless enemy who'd scale any slope
To ravage and devour what they wantonly desire.

Nowhere is entirely safe
From the murderer with a mission.

Not even in a city, with millions as witness,
High up in a great tower of steel and glass,
Is there refuge from the ruthless savage with wings and a prayer.

And as I descend from the ridge my feet tangle in bracken
And I stumble and fall and roll adeptly, like a log,
For protection. Only, my hip hits a stone.

Back on my feet, uninjured, I give a wry smile.
Is luck the safest of all havens?
Yet, as these ancient people showed, it's not enough
To depend on. It is wise to tread warily.

For even in those earlier days, instincts advised that
You guard against fate, not leave fate to guard you;
And if brutality, like a nightmare, appears unstoppable,
Compassion for the victim, the weak, the innocent,
At least keeps hope alive.

I've yet to find hard evidence about this reputed place of refuge, but it appeals and I empathise with victims threatened by evil, whatever their persuasion. September 11 and Palestine and Bali and Belfast – and all other places where wickedness prevails – are worthy of contempt.

As Dad
Sits smoking inside his Skoda,
Listening to the big match
On the car radio,
Mam
Cajoles her complaining kids
Along a beaten pathway
Towards the waterfall.

While he
Roars aloud in sudden rapture
As striker, Alan Shearer,
Heads in a leading goal,
She
Ponders gladly beside the pool,
Hearing their playful voices
Swirling above the stream.

When Dad
Gasps and grimaces in dismay,
As Sunderland equalise
In the dying minute,
Mam,
Sitting smoking upon a stone,
Happily catches her breath
In splashes of silver.

Later,
Driving home, harnessed and weary,
They peer out seeking to stop
For sweets and lottery.

The walk to Linhope Spout is a popular goal for many. We take from it what we seek.

Eerily,
Across the wasted grass,
A boulder, not a sheep,
Deceives the eye.

No less a torment
Than the jagged wind
Poking out a tear;
Or the child's pang:
"Why kill them all?"

Imprinted at the gateway,
The anguish of a last exit
Before their final assembly.

Systematic slaughter:

Officials, guns, tractors, loaders,
And then, piled high,
Soused with disinfectant,
Hearse-wagons leaking along
A crow-scavenged road
Towards a MAFF grave.

A site, no doubt,
Left unrecognised
By even the token
Of a single stone.

In August, 1966, our family farm at Swinhoe, Chathill, was infected by Foot and Mouth. I remember the gloom which beset the farming community then, as the burning dimmed our spirits. Only history will reveal the terrible cost of the 2001 plague. After culling, the deserted fields left the countryside looking bleak and forlorn, while the empty animal sheds remained silent and lifeless. Later reports that the disease, in the Milfield case, was not fully proven added further woe.

Bearded by pine trees,
The cave's wide mouth
Echoes, of an age
When the hunter or hunted,
Possessed or dispossessed,
Wearily sought shelter
From the open sky,
And the dark world
Outside and within themselves.

Weather-grimaced sandstone,
Where superficial declarations
Of presence or love
Are scratched
On the rock face,
While other mysterious traces,
Mutely shadowed,
Lie crouched deeper
In corners and cracks,
Less easily perceived.

Of course,
Only when childlike
Can such haunts be encountered,
Searching for clues
To the secrets of its past,
Coiled in the adventure
Of simple imaginings.

Only then,
In that spirit of mind
Does the cave whisper
To us, individually,
And the memorial of its being
May intone a sacred, blessed air.

*Hounded by Viking raiders, the monks finally deserted Lindisfarne in 875 and,
carrying Cuthbert's relics, set off on a journey which eventually led them to Durham.
At this cave they likely rested, or spent their first night. Today, nosing about its rocks
and recesses is fun and the mind fills with wonder at what might have been ... the
meetings, deals and conspiracies which may have taken place here.*

Escorted down from
Shepherd's Law,
Hands tied,
Some in silence,
Others with force,
They arrive at the tree.

Now,
Almost dead,
The old oak stands, still,
Beside the Hall;
The rusted wires
Of a child's swing
Hanging from broken bough.

Still standing,
The tree remains
A link with the past,
Bearing a history
Of pleasure and pain.
And now,
In silence,
Slowly dying,
The cries that once
Shook its branches
Lie hushed within.

A living relic to ponder beside, as a sinister reminder of how dreadful and summary justice must often have been in the past. The paradox of punishment and play speaks for itself.

Drab,
Two men stooping
Like herons in shallow water
Searching for eels.

The leader's sickle
Carving the sandy bed
As his companion captures
Any escaping downstream.

Far out,
The tide reveals a thin white wave,
Defining a beach
As empty as the pale, clear sky.

A bleak, chill, luminous setting,
Brushed by a merging of waters
And yellow sunlight,
Worthy of a Millet canvas.

A picture of calm, remote seascape,
Inhabited by elemental figures
Depicting form and outline,
Gleaned on a rare, December noon.

From a parked Alnwick Brewery wagon, eating sandwiches, the view was special.
'The Gleaners', by Millet, is a favourite painting.

Stiffened by fear and frost
A dead fox lies, woundless,
On a shawl of red soil.

Yesterday,
Against failing light,
Riders were seen skylined
Above the slope,
Trooping across
The moor's ribbed flank.

A score of centuries past,
Flight from savage, sworded hunters;
Blood of a saviour's birth,
And a death
That drips, even now,
From remorseless fangs.

Staring out over the Till's
Wide, dormant valley floor
Of Estate farmlands:
Akeld, Coupland, Ewart,
Fenton and beyond,
I stand, almost lifeless,

A stranger to my feelings
And all this I know
So well.

The next morning, Boxing Day, I returned with my two children to bury the young fox. It was a good enough reason for them to leave their new toys at home, if only for a short while. I told them the animal had died of a heart attack, which it likely had.

A mild, sunny spring afternoon.
As my boy and his pal hunt newts, toads,
Frogs and spawn round a peat-stained pond,
I overlook the vale where only yesterday
Our school cycle group passed through.

Away, below Hedgehope, a smear of smoke
From burning heather. Behind me on the moor
Skylarks flutter in song. Down in the fields,
First lambs totter and laze beside ewes.
From Beanley kennels the light breeze
Carries the whiff of hounds.

Lately, news has not been good.

A friend and his wife about to part;
Over the Tweed, a young man dead from
His own gun; a neighbour in Wooler
Condemned by ill-health.

Glumly, I remain, doubts clashing
Against this show of early spring;
Nature's change, country life, childhood ways.
And once more I am astounded by this body
Of land; its firm, gentle edges, its slow
Breath of space and silent heartbeat
Urging, in a murmur, to withstand
And enjoy.

The Breamish, meaning 'bright water', flows out of Ingram valley and trails northwards becoming the river Till at Bewick Mill bridge. This cradle of land advancing towards the Scottish border is celebrated for its charm, particularly on stunning viewing days, which the poem highlights. As an optimist, I constantly need an affirmation to outweigh the lows which inevitably shadow life. The wonder of my homeland does this for me.

Concealed in willows,
Peter the artist
Paints his picture;
The rusted tors
Straddling a cleft
Of hills.

Above their knuckles,
He chalks a paler blue
To edge their mould,
Rippling their slopes
Of underlying green
With scrubs of burnt,
Livid bronze.
Using blackened shadows
He stirs and swells
A slash of lower pines;
Then, dusting a faint
Yellow ochre over
Creased, upper folds,
He attempts the motion
Of a hazed, mystical light.

Secluded in shelter,
Peter the artist
Aspires earnestly towards
An aura of shape and mood,
Inexorably bearing
The inner forces
Of uncertain calm.

For Peter, a lover of opera; a rather weighty portrayal of his art in its endless quest for meaning and understanding. Creativity is an act, a personal struggle between the need to express and the ability to satisfy that. The twin tors are symbolic of this two-headed monster.

Cheviot Charlie, phantom shepherd, traipsing
Into Wooler from his haunt in the hills.
Scarecrow figure, face ruddy as heather,

Parading, peddling the image of old rustic fool.
Rough in appearance, like wind-blown bracken,
Worn, shaggy, wild; cheering dull heads.

Pleasing the crowd with drawling verses,
Rolling rhymes; a broad native tongue.
His coarse accent jewelled by local dialect,
Harping the air, like the lone curlew's cry.

Teller of tales: humour, pity, wonder.
Championing the romance of bygone days,
Where canny folks readily shared in fortune
And toil, and home fiddles strove to kittle the heart.

Revelling merrily from throng to throng,
His spell quaint as a painted clown's.
Nature's droll jester, moulded from seasons,

Bred with wisdom howked from peat-clad earth.
Comic myth-maker, revealing in guise how
A simple soul serves, shaping virtue from fun.

or many years as a practical joker, George Ridpeath, alias Cheviot Charlie, dressed up
disguise to entertain crowds with his philosophical and fanciful renditions. On the
uter wall of the Rendezvous Café in Wooler, his effigy hangs, reinforcing his image in
cal folklore.

Wind-warped trees on the crest of the hillside
Clustered round the Old Moor Inn.
Pocked and gouged by hooves and cart-wheels,
A rough road clambers up towards a thick,
Grained, wooden door.

In the flame-lit room of smoked, stone walls,
A traveller and pedlar sit waiting to be served,
Bread, broth and ale. A dithering woman, apron grubby,
Wipes crumbs from the table as a hound creeps by.

"The' say the' caught the highwayman on Thrunton Crag,
late yesterday, 'fore dusk fell," says she.
The traveller nods. "Aye, at Wedderburn's Hole, so I
was told by hind folk, as I rode up Whittingham Lane."

The pedlar spits into the sea coal fire, then dries
His mouth on a tattered sleeve. "Cuckoo not yet, Peg,"
he croaks. "Maybe the devil might save him again!"
She turns to grin. "Man, Aa doubt he'll get away
this time, for he's a'ready shackled at Callaly."

"So the strife he's caused shall soon be ended! Tell me,
woman," the other demands, "when does the scoundrel hang?"
"Ah sir, as soon as a rope's wrapped round his neck!"
she cackles drily, a besom shank clutched in her hand.

The traveller stares. "Oh, indeed! Then a half-wit woman with
an idle mouth should know, if he has family left to mourn?"
The pedlar, head bent forward like a toad's, grunts aloud,
"No more, the' say, than what's covered by his hat!"

In silence, they hear a burst of rain pelting the roof;
The chimney yowls in a sudden gust.
Slouched beneath the table, the dog lifts its head,
Glares at the fall of soot, then yawns.

The foundations of the old inn and the ride through the trees give a clear impression of the highway as it must have looked. Known robbers frequented this lonesome stretch and the atmosphere of the place is well worth sampling. Peg Macfarlane was a besom-maker's daughter, widely known in the district as a dither.

Rumbustious country lads,
Red-faced with summer sun,
And girls, eyes bright and happy,
All out to have some fun.
The smell of steaks cooking,
Smoke drifting overhead,
Mike Hope's disco booming,
Loud voices filling the shed.
Boys from Thropton and Glanton
Seem ready for a fight,
But Kenny Davidson's humour
Puts everything to rights.
A lass from up the valley,
Sick with rum and Coke,
Is helped out to a jeep
And wrapped up in a coat.
Dancing crazy as a clown,
Young Frankie Walton beams,
As Snaith and Swordy gape at
Girls in tight-fit jeans.

While Musk got fixed-up early,
Me, I had no luck at all,
Then I went and lost a fiver
To add injury to a fall.
My steak was burnt and stringy,
Almost impossible to chew,
And someone spilled their beer
On my Nature Trekker shoes.
In the car home I decided
I'd not be back next year,
Unless I got invited
By the girl with corn-gold hair.

It's true – ask anybody who used to go! Apologies to those named.

Too many flowers
For the vase
At the window.

Gazing out
Across the vale,
A bright, blue-soaked
May morning.

A shower running;
Soft, pale curves
Glisten beneath
The spray of the rose.

Deserving care,
Love, like flowers,
Circulates the heart,
Illuminates a smile.

Rising
Above the river's mist
The stretched back of Simonside
Lifts the sky.

A familiar view from Pondicherry; continually changing and always captivating.

Slumped in his armchair beside the hearth,
Fire flameless, hardly glowing.
Alone in the gloom he stares at the window,
Curtains still open.

Above the sombre stone of the village cross
Where eighteen names are inscribed in honour,
The moon lies on its back, like a tilted grin.

He sees her face, hears her whisper
Of others in uniform about to depart.
With a cast of hand he insists they enter,
Pull back the mats, drink, sing and dance;
But already they're fading, waving farewell.
Stamping a tune, he calls out their names,
Heart beating faster, remembering their youth,
Reckless of the night and spell of shadows,
The menace of a witch's leering moon,
Straining him into silence, a strange,
Confounding silence.

Outside, his dog begins to whine.
Uncertain now, he hauls himself onto his feet,
Staggers through the door, switching on the light.
In the back kitchen he peers through the window.

Suddenly, across his chest, a blast of pain.
His legs give way but he clasps the basin,
Refusing to fall he clings to life,
For the triumph of it, keeps holding on;
Beaten but not broken shall endure the night,
Staying on his feet he gains, at last, a final say.

*'Keep a hold' is a common Northumbrian expression. Bob Fairbairn did just that.
Strangely, his dog was found dead in its kennel the same morning. This coincidence –
and the manner of Bob's dying, which befitted his hardy nature – was for me a powerful
image.*

Behind the wood
Mist gathers like
A ghostly flock.
In wheel ruts
Pools of rainwater
Tremble in a chill breeze.
Clouds spilling
Across the western sky
Cloak Cheviot's top.
Hanging on fence wire
A chorus line of dead crows
Sway together in
A grim finale.

Upon a small mound
In a nearby field
A circle of five
Standing stones
Like old wizened teeth
Flute the wind;
An anthem to
Forgotten Gods.

Approaching the small stone circle you are immediately absorbed by its simple splendour. Moving around the stones, you are drawn to touch them. Under a dark, wild, winter sky their shapes have an unearthly, awesome aspect; something I have tried to evoke in the poem.

Holding his heels
As he looks for a ledge,
I bore his weight
Longer than was comfortable.
He managed the climb.

On cold, grey, granite rocks
We tested our skills;
Nothing severe, without ropes,
But enough to be achieved.

On Cheviot's edge,
Where woodrush grows
And heather and moss
Lie paled by wind and snow,
I strode down with him;
A tall, white-haired,
Noble figure;
Face sharp and lean
As a harrier's.

Enthused by venture and nature,
I look up yet,
Holding him
In respect.

Almost forty years separated us, as well as a life which seemed a world apart. But when we went on these occasional outings, we shared a common interest and enjoyment of the hills and the climbs. Lord Howick later fell from a crag near his home and died, in March, 1973. The Henhole is named after the bird – the hen harrier – which at one time nested in the ravine.

At the end of my run
I stop at the bridge
And step down to the river's edge.

Kneeling over the clear
Cold water I splash off
The sweat stinging my face.

A mere mile up stream, beneath
The dome of Yeavering Bell,
Paulinus from Kent baptised
The first Northumbrian converts,
In 627.

Afterwards,
Standing on the grassy bank,
As they must have done,
Head and hands still dripping,
I feel refreshed and calm,
Uplifted by a sense of well-being.

Like leaping fish, drawn
From below the rippled surface
Into air, they too, infused by
A prospect of change and light,
Were encouraged to haul themselves,
Higher than me, above the murky,
Stoney shallows of a restless,
Improbable world.

The effort to run and the rewarding contentment and peace of mind it usually brings is compared and contrasted here with that of the greater commitment and dedication of those converts to the new faith of Christianity, which King Edwin permitted and which a little later, in Oswald's reign, resulted in the founding of the monastery on Lindisfarne, in 635.

Slammed down,
His body lay broken
Across the track,
His eyes, gaping,
Branded by the shock
Of instant pain.

Not far away,
On a field's rise,
John Bannan lies buried
Like some worthy Lord
In safe seclusion;
Every passing train
Seen and heard.

Above
The root-tilted grave,
Two trees tower,
Their sparse branches
Unfurled like flags,
In opposite directions;
A shrouded signal,
Either towards
His wasteful death,
Or the affection
Fellow workers felt
They owed.

n iron cross marks the grave of John Bannan, an Irish 'navvy', believed to have been
lled at work on the line near Christon Bank, September 19th, 1854. Another account
as him as a farm worker who fell through a granary floor and, being a Catholic, was
nable to be buried in the local churchyard. Whatever the truth, for him to be buried in
uch an honourable way suggests he was greatly regarded.
he late Geoff Stephenson's photographs originally stimulated the idea of
ccompanying this collection of poetry with images. It is a privilege to include this one.

Afoot ...

You know, not too long ago my father could take a journey around north Northumberland and name practically every farm, and who farmed there. Some of the farm names are worth uttering aloud: Whistlebare, Glororum, Kypie, Snableazes, Dancing Hall, Overgrass, Mount Hooley, Wisplaw and many more. There's an old rhyme which uses names of farms located beyond Kirknewton and, regardless of other versions, goes something like this ...

Raised a hare at Canno Mill
Chased it over Bowmont Hill
Downed it at Downham
Shot it at Shotton
Killed it at Kilham
And e't it at Yetholm

Many of the old farming families are still here, too: the Snaiths, Telfords, Brewises, Currys, Fraters, Bells, Murrays, Greens, Shells, Reavleys, Rogersons, Robsons, and so forth. I like it. There's something permanent and reassuring about it.

If you stand on a hilltop, especially on Ros Castle above Chillingham, you can view, with a turn of the head, most of this area of land, wedged between the sea and border hills. Because I am part of it – I belong here – I feel proud and privileged. I was born here, I live here, I'll probably die here. It's home.

In my poetry there is, hopefully, an almost physical presence of place, as well as a knowledge which only comes from personal experience. Each location, on a particular day and in its own way, left a lasting impression which stirred my imagination. The eel catchers, at their patient task in 'Alnmouth Estuary', effectively drew their own picture in my mind's eye. It could have been John, in his wheelchair at Waterside House across the river, woodcrafting with his powerful hands, or even boyhood memories of old Brown, the boatman, who earned a little money rowing folks across the water. There was, too, the drowning of the Galbraith boy, swept out to sea, which shocked us all terribly. However, in 'Aln Estuary', it simply turned out to be the river's gleaners.

Places like Cuthbert's Cave, Lindisfarne, Duddo, Yeavering, Flodden, Rimside, Blawearie, and many like them, all possess their own atmosphere, threaded with history, mystery and, indeed, romance. Looking closely at them, and their settings, against the sky and earth, my imagination readily wandered into the past and I was excited by the sense of danger, isolation and glory they inspired. Lingering with them in silence, I wanted to save something of that, and the words which would eventually form these poems were, in a sense, my way of painting them.

A friend, Peter Podmore, an artist living at West Newton, stares daily at the hills. Behind his gaze he searches for an idea that excites him and which he can develop in his work. The actual view is merely a starting point for his own vision. Intrigued by his work, and in order to fathom his efforts, I needed to put myself in his shoes so to speak, grappling to look into one of his paintings which hangs on a wall at home. My conclusions helped form the poem, 'West Newton'.

Characters like Bob Fairbairn, Lyall Thompson, Jack Douglas and other working men had strong qualities that were not difficult for me to admire as well. They were good company and good fun; all of them eager to work and live. My liking for them was natural. Although Lord Howick came from another background, he was similar to them in many ways; an outdoors man, energetic and enthusiastic about life. I didn't know who he was at first, when we'd pass each other in the woods at Howick, stopping to chat briefly. He learned I liked to climb too, and was keen to arrange a day, then later, others. I felt at ease in his company and since both of us were fond of a good Western film, we shared another interest also.

In Kenya, where he had been Governor, he had risked his life saving one of two drowning women, and his own health suffered as a consequence of the strain. It was the act of a man of ability and conscience; unlike cowboys of the screen, he was a real hero.

'Below Flodden', the title poem of this collection, was stimulated by another special individual, Andrew Patton, who farmed at the Linthaugh, Ford. In Northumberland's Foot and Mouth year of 1966, he was President of the Northumberland Farmers' Union. He had also been one of the first soldiers to enter Belsen concentration camp when it was liberated, towards the end of World War II. I have seen a few of his photographs showing some of the slaughter and degradation of its prisoners. The irony of himself, a war-worn old man, living and working in the shadow of Flodden hill beside the timeless vein of the river Till, struck a deep note – and a realisation – which led me to write the poem.

For me, the battle of Flodden continues to dominate the whole of the Till valley. It was an immensely bloody affair, which still haunts the Borders today, nearly five hundred years afterwards. The solemn monument at Branxton, unveiled by Sir George Douglas, Bart., on September 27th, 1910, and the respect of visitors paying tribute to the thousands who were slain, is evidence of that; none more poignant than the annual wreath of homage carried to the battle site, every August, by the Coldstreamer, at the border town's annual ride out during their civic week.

The impact of this battle resounds yet in fact and myth. The writing of 'Branxton Field' was my attempt to depict the personal terror of simple soldiers, something usually ignored in military accounts of the fight.

Conflict has, of course, enriched the history of this region. The invading forces of Romans, Angles, Danes, Saxons, Normans and Scots have all effected change, leaving traces that are visible today. What other small area of land in this country contains as much fortification? Battles, skirmishes and raids seem to echo over every stretch of ground. How lawless and fearful it must have been, at times, for ordinary folk. During the age of the Reiver, this was 'Wild West' territory, for sure!

Percy's fatal leap at Wooperton ended the battle of Hedgeley. Though not on a grand scale like Flodden, it was important and entered into folklore, as did the skirmish at Humbleton in 1402, involving the famed Percy, Harry Hotspur, and which is discussed at the beginning of Shakespeare's King Henry IV, Part One. In 'Percy's Leap', the idea of lining up Andy Scott, the older, with Sir Richard is speculative, but not without some credibility. In today's local folklore, there are plenty of stories of Andy's toughness and obdurate nature. Injury, discomfort or foul weather rarely succeeded in preventing him from setting out to work. Foolhardy, one might even have said of him at times, but in business he certainly proved himself no fool!

For me, reading tales of events, characters and places in the locality is an enjoyable way of understanding and learning more about them. Books like Dippie Dixon's *Whittingham Vale* and *Upper Coquetdale* provide a valuable source. Also, in August 1983, when I pedalled around the county for a week on a three-geared, rust-rattling, dirty old bike, I carried the marvellous Arthur Mee's *King's England* book on Northumberland.

But even better than any literature is the excitement of first-hand information, which comes through talking to individuals who are directly – or indirectly – linked to the subject. Such door-to-door research into the past relies much upon one's curiosity and courtesy.

Blawearie, a ruined shepherd's cottage on the moor above Old Bewick, like many others, creaks with stories of its past life. It was just such curiosity which led me to speak with descendents of the Rogerson and Rutherford families. Their information helped to confirm and shape the poem. Connections like this provided real insight, and added colour to my mental sketch of how it might have been when lived in and 'breathing'. Ken Smith's evocative photograph was taken in the mid-1980s. Since then the roof has collapsed and the structure is slowly shrinking. I first visited Blawearie in 1963 as an eighteen-year-old and, each time I return, its appeal is just as strong.

In 1946, aged twenty-two, Fritz Bertheli of Heburn came, via a Prisoner Of War camp in the United States, to a similar camp in Wooler where Glendale School is now situated. The camp held German and Italian prisoners, who were taken out to local farms to work. After the war, a few like Fritz remained, to marry local girls, work and live. For his later services to forestry, Fritz was awarded the British Empire Medal (I do believe the only other German-born UK citizen to receive the award was ex-Manchester City goalkeeper, Bert Trautmann). Fritz's outstanding finds of prehistoric artefacts are displayed as a collection in Chillingham Castle. His help was necessary in providing basic authenticity in the writing of 'POW Camp 105, Wooler'.

Naturally, in my poetry, imagination is the overriding feature – not fact, but a sense of truth is meant to grace them. The 'Lindisfarne' poem I began after an enjoyable stroll around the island with my brother Danny, who offered snatches of 'inside' information, whereas 'Old Bewick' was done and dusted before Brenda Brodie, of Milfield, confirmed what had actually happened to the girls.

In my 'Rimside' poem, the fiction makes use of characters that I felt were likely to have assembled there. A vivid imagination was certainly necessary to capture the spirit of the place. For years now, when teaching drama, I've used the inn as a scene wherein an ally of the highwayman manages to delay his hanging; hence the nature of the poem's dialogue. However, some things can't be made up! For instance, Bob Fairbairn dying on his feet, the P.O.W.s' rotating bed-places in their hut, Fleming beneath a portrait of the Queen, a football blown away, mother forgetting the potatoes, picking crab apples with my children, Colin on his pony, Thomas in his boat – and others – were all real occurrences which stayed with me, and springboarded a need to write and make something more of them.

What some have remarked upon as my boyish sense of adventure has, through the years, prompted hundreds of outings across the surrounding countryside. The sheer pleasure of walking, running and cycling over that ground, and getting to know it better, has always been an easy joy for me. When I was young, remaining in the house for any great length of time always felt to me like a punishment, and it still does.

Just, as is said, the best manure on a farm is the farmer's own footsteps, so following the river, crossing the moor, climbing the hill, is the only way to really appreciate them. What's more, I've found that exploring with an interested mind adds so much more to the experience. Cuthbert's Cave is a lot larger and more magical if, as you scramble about it, you dwell upon its previous visitors – and uses – down the ages.

Accompanying people who possess a wealth of local knowledge, like my brother Danny and friends Jimmy Givens and Fred Dyson, I can always learn something new. When I head out alone, however, there are fewer distractions and a silence with the power to free the imagination. By nature, I like company but I'm happy enough to go out alone, and in remote spots that seems somehow fitting. Oddly enough, however, in such situations I often have the urge to speak out loud. Indeed, since childhood, whenever alone I seem to have occupied my head with dreams and wonders, and then attempted to talk them out. Anyone overhearing one of these one-sided conversations would fear for my sanity!

Despite the changes and development brought about by modern life, the presence of a solitary landscape still remains within easy reach of village and town. Winter highlights this more powerfully, as some of the accompanying photographs in this volume show. In a similar way, the meagre lines of my poem 'Gain's Law' are intended to mirror a scene of barren desolation.

On our doorstep, as it were, the Cheviot hills provide freedom and escape for the venturer, something I hope the 'Harthope' poem manages to evoke in the reader. Even from as far away as the coast, the Cheviots stand out across the countryside, defining where we live. Throughout my own life here in north Northumberland, they have always been on the horizon, a territorial edge, a bleak boundary that affirms the area's sense of its own identity, and makes it, for me, a special place. Returning from my travels, I feel I'm back home the moment they come into view.

Whatever the Cheviot hills lack in terms of size and mass, they more than compensate with their bounty of picturesque beauty and frontier legend. Still clearly recognisable, prehistoric camps, Roman routes, raiders' pathways, drove roads, smugglers' and hunters' crossings display an air of threat and romance which anyone today can easily visualise. Added to this, despite their gently rolling appearance, the truth remains that the Cheviot hills can prove deadly in foul weather, claiming lives. Stories of tragedy and calamity are numerous ...

Almost to the day, ninety-nine years after Nellie Herron perished on Prendwick Moor, in December, 1863, two shepherds – Middlemist and Scott – failed to make the journey from Alnham to Ewartly Shank, overcome by a terrible blizzard, roughly a mile from Nellie Herron's Stone. And it was only in February, 1988, that a snow avalanche killed two walkers in The Bizzle ravine, above Dunsdale. Aeroplane crashes in the Cheviots are extensively listed in Peter Clark's book, *Where The Hills Meet The Sky*, and the graves of young airmen in St Gregory's churchyard at

Kirknewton serve as a stark reminder of the dangers and wasted lives.

It was, of course, on Hepburn Moor that the shepherd and his wife from Old Botany were lost, searching for a missing cow, and which shapes the ending of my 'Blawearie' poem. Nowadays, life for people living in remote parts is nowhere near as difficult or hazardous as it once was, but even so a battery of gales or blizzards is no less intimidating. In out-by situations the possibility of being blocked in by snow for days – or weeks – is very real.

There's an old story about a grandmother's death in such an isolated spot which makes sense of this. Since it was impossible to transport her body out of the valley, her family wrapped it up and buried it in a snow drift to prevent it decomposing. Later, when conditions improved and the road was passable, she was shovelled out from her freezer bed and carted down for a proper funeral.

As the reader may well have noticed, many of my poems are concerned with loss, and my response to it. Death's piercing touch usually digs deepest into our emotions. After Susan Maxwell's terrible fate in August, 1982, the whole area was stunned beyond belief that such an evil deed could occur, and here. It immediately resulted in a drastic shift in attitude in every local parent. Suddenly it was no longer the safe place they thought it to be. For everyone locally who remembers the crime, the heart shudders a little yet, each time we cross over the bridge at Coldstream.

Caring – and not caring – were the underlying factors in writing 'For Susan'. Acts of kindness and insensitivity cut across our lives. Those who live wholly according to their good intentions are rare. Jack Douglas, the shepherd, cared for animals that were bred for killing. He was not confused by it. He managed them sympathetically and was rational about their fate. He was a warm, humble and decent being. A gentleman in the true sense.

Living on a farm as a youth, I recall whacking down sparrows with a tennis racket while standing on the main beam in the old granary. They were a pest and it was a good enough reason for a laugh. It didn't seem wrong, then. Yet, at the same age, I spilled tears when our old labrador had to be put down.

After leaving school and returning home, work on the farm – plus the books of John Steinbeck and H E Bates – encouraged in me a closer interest in nature and its seasons. And then, almost singly, shooting a dove in mistake for a wood pigeon shocked my conscience and prompted a cause for growing up. For a while after that, caring became a holy ambition, as only youth knows how.

The 'Red Steads' poem emerged from a startling half-hour of sun after rain. My eyes were wide open and I was excited by the world, with the farm as its centre and everything connected to it. In writing about the shepherd, Jack Douglas, my idea was to weave the routine action of checking sheep with the turning of the year – and his lifetime. Later, in 'Lyall Thompson', the yearly wheel continues to grind out the days. Lyall died in 1996, but the sound of a mell hammering in posts still rings through the year, continuing the motion that started, for me, at Red Steads.

The stride of time lies majestically over this countryside, as places like Duddo Stones and Yeavering Bell testify. It is sombre and remarkable. In these personal writings I rejoice in the auras of the past, near and far. The immediate attractions of the area are important but, despite a glorious history and an imposing landscape, without the fibre of its individual characters and communities, the place – like some others – might rapidly lose its vitality and simply become … a museum, dulled by empty holiday homes, silent village schools, vacant shops and post offices. I know I'm not alone in my fears of these effects upon north Northumberland. This following piece, wryly titled 'Remember Bamburgh' reflects my concerns.

Stone by stone the old mill is taken down.
Across the stream rows of burning straw
Roll out thick grey columns of smoke.
On a dead elm a woodpecker hammers
The ragged bark.

Images grow, overlap and merge;
Bale by bale a building of straw rises up.
Under cover, winter logs are stored.
Within walls, the scuffle of birds,
Seeking shelter.

Only in dream can rubble and ash
Have creation.
Only with mind can that which is lost
Remain
Only by vision can a world worth saving
Be secure.

I suppose it's mainly by chance that we live at all. What later inspires and paves our routes through life is reflected in the theme lying behind the 'Old Bewick' poem. It was only through chance that I discovered the girls' grave and, as on other such forays, I was reminded of just how lucky I am to be alive, and with the energy to enjoy these encounters. With my life firmly tied to north Northumberland I feel an instinctive need to connect with it, not merely physically but perhaps spiritually, too. This can happen by design as well as accident, and I hope the rewards are expressed in poems like 'Breamish Vale'.

The writing of them has often proven the hardest part of all. Sometimes when wrestling for words, I almost believe it would be simpler to haul a wheelbarrow up to the top of Cheviot; at least I would be certain of the way. Fortunately, however, for a long time I have had the wisdom of Fred Dyson, of Alnwick, to advise me. Since those early poetry meetings in a little sideroom of The Tanner's Arms, where the ringing of a small handbell would summon Jack McKenzie, the landlord, Fred's guidance has remained inspirational throughout these and many other efforts.

My father, to pay off a loan from his father, undertook contract work in addition to running his own farm. This also enabled him to get to know the area as well as he did. Ironically, I reckon my efforts, journeying across this same countryside – and writing about it – are as much about being prepared to roll up my sleeves as were his. Since my grandfather, whom I never met, accepted the repayment – then handed it back, satisfied that his son had shown through his labour all that was needed, I'd like to think my late father, in his droll manner, might have acknowledged generously my own exertions here with this collection.

You know, I've always felt that the true glory is in the effort; that it's trying that really counts. I believe our minds are full of rivers on which we carry thoughts and, by trying, I found a river I like to follow again and again. Returning to it is an act of faith, a desire to respect the blessing of what has passed, and is passing now. For me, time spent below Flodden is worth every bit of love.

POEMS

All photographs by Ken Smith except:

For Susan, Linhope Spout and Shadow Over Milfield
by Jimmy Keen.

Alnham Church, Cheviot Charlie and Rimside Moor
by Bob Smith.

Flotterton Barbecue: Mike Hope.

Paddy's Mount courtesy of Mrs Geoff Stephenson.

Howick Hole, Lyall Thompson, A Great Love, Skirl Naked, The
Village King, Chatton Bank Cottage, Yeavering Bell, Harthope
Valley, Jack Douglas, Maidens' Chambers, Death Of An Old Man
and The Glen At Ewart by the author.

Front cover photograph by Ken Smith.

Rear cover photograph by the author.